Table of Contents

Introduction

Chapter 1: Tips to Balance the Books.

1.1 Understand Your Financial Statements.
1.2 Implement Effective Budgeting.
1.3 Monitor Cash Flow.

Chapter 2: Tips to Succeed in Business.

2.1 Define Your Unique Selling Proposition (USP).

2.2 Build Strong Customer Relationships.

2.3 Embrace Innovation.

Chapter 3: Tips to Win in the Financial Industry.

3.1 Stay Informed.

3.2 Develop a Strong Professional Network.

3.3 Continuously Enhance Your Skills.

Summary.

Introduction:

Welcome to "Mastering Profit and Loss: Top Tips for Financial Success."

In this eBook, we will explore essential strategies and techniques to help you balance the books, succeed in business, and thrive in the financial industry.

Whether you are an entrepreneur, a business owner, or an aspiring professional, these tips will provide you with valuable insights to enhance your financial acumen and drive profitability.

By implementing these proven methods, you can increase your profitability, make informed financial decisions, and achieve long-term success So, let's dive in and unlock the secrets to financial success!

CHAPTER 1: TIPS TO BALANCE THE BOOKS

1.1 **Understand Your Financial Statements**:

Learn how to interpret and analyse income statements balance sheets, and cash flow statements to gain a comprehensive understanding of your financial position.

Understanding your financial statements is essential for managing your finances effectively and making informed decisions about your personal or business finances.

Financial statements provide a snapshot of your financial health and help you track your income, expenses, assets, and liabilities over a specific period.

There are three primary types of financial statements: the income statement, the balance sheet, and the cash flow statement.

Here is an overview of each financial statement and what it reveals about your financial situation.

Income Statement:

1. The income statement, also known as the profit and loss statement, shows your revenue, expenses, and net income or loss over a specific period, typically a month, quarter, or year.

2. It provides an overview of how much money you earned (revenue) and how much you spent (expenses) to generate that revenue.

3. The net income is calculated by subtracting total expenses from total revenue and indicates whether you made a profit or incurred a loss during the period.

4. Analysing the income statement can help you identify trends in your income and expenses, assess your profitability, and adjust improve your financial performance. Looking into the income statement in more details, you will have a clearer understanding and will be confident to used it effectively.

5. Revenue is the total amount of money earned from sales, services, or other sources of income. It represents the top line of the income statement and is a crucial indicator of your businesses or personal financial performance.

6. Expenses are the costs incurred to generate revenue and operate the business. Expenses can include salaries, rent, utilities, supplies, marketing expenses, and other operating costs.

7. Gross Profit is calculated by subtracting the cost of goods sold from total revenue. It reflects the profitability of the core business operations before considering other expenses.

8. Net Income also known as the bottom line, is the amount left after deducting all expenses from revenue. It indicates the overall profitability of the business or individual after accounting for all costs.

Balance Sheet:

1. The balance sheet provides a snapshot of your assets, liabilities, and equity at a specific point in time, usually the end of a reporting period.

2. It shows what you own (assets), what you owe (liabilities), and the difference between the two (equity).

3. Assets include cash, investments, real estate, inventory, and equipment, while liabilities include debts, loans, and other financial obligations.

4. Equity represents the difference between assets and liabilities and reflects the net worth of the individual or business.

The balance sheet helps you assess your financial position, liquidity, and solvency, and evaluate how effectively you are managing your assets and liabilities.

Assets are items of value owned by the business or individual, such as cash, investments, accounts receivable, inventory, equipment, and property. Assets are categorized as current assets (e.g., cash and accounts receivable) and non-current assets (e.g., property and equipment), whiles Liabilities are debts and obligations owed by the business or individual to external parties, such as loans, accounts payable, and accrued expenses. Liabilities are classified as current liabilities (e.g., short-term debts) and non-current liabilities (e.g., long-term loans).

Equity represents the owner's stake in the business or individual's net worth. It is calculated as the difference between assets and liabilities and includes retained earnings, contributions from owners, and other equity components.

Cash Flow Statement:

The cash flow statement shows how cash flows in and out of your business over a specific period, categorizing cash inflows and outflows into operating, investing, and financing activities.

It helps you track the sources and uses of cash, assess your ability to generate cash, and evaluate your liquidity and financial health.

The cash flow statement is crucial for understanding your cash position, identifying cash flow problems, and planning for future cash needs.

when looking at cash flow statements in more detail you'll notice that

1. Cash flows from operating activities include cash receipts and payments related to the core business operations, such as sales, purchases, and operating expenses. Positive operating cash flow indicates that the business is generating sufficient cash from its operations.
2. Cash flows from investing activities involve cash transactions related to the acquisition and disposal of long-term assets, such as property, equipment, and investments. Investing cash flow reflects the business's investment in growth and capital expenditures.

3. Cash flows from financing activities include cash transactions related to borrowing, repaying debt, issuing equity, and paying dividends. Financing cash flow shows how the business is funding its operations and capital structure.

By understanding and analysing your financial statements, you can gain valuable insights into your financial performance, make informed decisions, and take proactive steps to improve your financial well-being. these financial statements in conjunction with each other allows you can gain a comprehensive understanding of your financial position, performance, and cash flow dynamics. This information is vital for making strategic decisions, identifying areas for improvement, and ensuring financial stability and growth.

1.2 Implement Effective Budgeting:

Discover the importance of creating a realistic budget and how it can help you track expenses, control costs, and optimize your financial resources.

Implementing effective budgeting and monitoring cash flow are essential practices for managing your finances efficiently and ensuring financial stability. The key steps with budgeting within your business are defining your short-term and long-term financial goals, whether it's saving for a major purchase, paying off debt, or building an emergency fund. Your goals will guide your budgeting efforts.

1. Create a Budget by developing a comprehensive budget that outlines your income, expenses, and savings goals. Allocate specific amounts to different expense categories, such as housing, utilities, groceries, transportation, and entertainment.

2. Track your spending and monitor your expenses regularly to ensure that you are staying within your budget limits. Use budgeting tools, apps, or spreadsheets to track your spending and identify areas where you can cut costs or reallocate funds.

3. Prioritize saving by allocating a portion of your income to savings and investments to build a financial cushion and achieve your long-term goals. Consider setting up automatic transfers to your savings account to ensure consistent savings.

4. Review and adjust your budget periodically to assess your progress towards your goals and adjust as needed. Be flexible and willing to adapt your budget based on changing circumstances or financial priorities.

Here are also a few extra Budgeting Strategies that you can apply, I have broken these down in more detail to ensure you have a full understanding of the context.

1. Categorize Expenses by dividing your expenses into categories such as fixed expenses (e.g., rent, utilities), variable expenses (e.g., groceries, dining out), debt payments, savings, and discretionary spending. This categorization helps you prioritize and manage your expenses effectively.

2. Set Realistic Targets to Establish realistic spending for each expense category based on your income and financial goals. Be mindful of your financial limitations and avoid overspending in areas that are not aligned with your priorities.

3. Consider using the envelope system where you allocate cash to specific envelopes for different expense categories. This method helps you visually track your spending and prevents overspending by limiting yourself to the cash in each envelope.

4. Track Expenses Regularly this allows you to Keep a close eye on your expenses, by tracking them regularly you will have an idea whether daily, weekly, or monthly what you're spending. Use budgeting apps, spreadsheets, or financial tracking tools to monitor your spending and identify any deviations from your budget.

5. Regularly review your budget and compare your actual spending to your budgeted amounts. Analyse your spending patterns, identify areas where you can cut back or reallocate funds, and make adjustment to stay on track with your financial goals.

Monitor Cash Flow:

Track Cash Inflows and Monitor all sources of income, including salaries, business revenue, investments, and other sources of cash inflow. Keep track of when payments are received to ensure a steady cash flow.

1. Monitor Cash Outflows and Track your expenses, including fixed costs (e.g., rent, utilities) and variable costs (e.g., groceries, entertainment). Identify areas where you can reduce expenses or optimize spending to improve cash flow.

2. Forecast Cash Needs and Anticipate upcoming expenses, such as bills, loan payments, and other financial obligations. Create a cash flow forecast to project your future cash inflows and outflows and plan accordingly.

3. Maintain Adequate Reserves and Build up an emergency fund to cover unexpected expenses or income disruptions. Having a financial buffer can help you avoid cash flow problems and financial stress during challenging times.

4. Consider using cash flow management tools or software to streamline the tracking and analysis of your cash flow. These tools can provide insights into your cash position and help you make informed financial decisions.

Implementing these cash flow monitoring practices, you can gain better control over your finances, improve your financial health, and work towards achieving your financial goals also consistent monitoring and proactive financial management will help you navigate uncertainties and maintain financial stability over time.

As you've now get a hang of monitoring cash flow let's delve deeper into a few effective strategies for monitoring cash flow.

Cash Flow Monitoring Strategies:

Cash flow statement helps you visualize how cash moves in and out of your accounts and identify potential cash flow issues.

1. By Analysing your cash flow patterns to understand when your income peaks and dips and when your expenses are highest. This insight can help you anticipate cash flow challenges and plan accordingly to ensure sufficient liquidity.

2. Build Cash Reserves by aiming to maintain adequate cash reserves to cover your expenses and financial obligations in case of unexpected emergencies or income disruptions. Having a buffer of savings can provide financial security and peace of mind.

3. Negotiate favourable payment terms with suppliers, vendors, or creditors to align payment deadlines with your cash flow cycle. Request extended payment terms or explore instalment options to manage cash flow more effectively.

4. Monitor Receivables and Payables by keeping track of accounts receivable to ensure timely collection of payments from customers or clients. Similarly, manage accounts payable by scheduling payments strategically to optimize cash flow and maintain positive vendor relationships.

Cash Flow Statement:

Operating Activities	Amount
Cash payment from Clients	£2,150,000
Payment for Inventory	(840,000)
Payment for Salaries	(408,000)
Payment for Rent	(190,000)
Payment for Advertising	(162,000)
Payment for income taxes	(104,000)
Payment for insurance	(114,000)
Total Cash inflow from Operating Activities	£332,000
Investment Activities	
Cash received from sales of business	52,000

Cash received from sale of land	150,000
Cash received in purchased of houses	(600,000)
Total Cash outflow from Investment Activities	(66,000)
Cash Flow from Financing Activities	
Cash received from bank on a loan	240,000
Cash paid as dividends	(200,000)
Total Cash inflow from Financing Activities	£40,000
Cash Reduction throughout the year	(34,000)
Cash Balance -January 2024	78,000
Cash Balance - December 2024	£44,000

Monitoring cash flow is crucial for maintaining financial stability and ensuring that you have enough liquidity to cover your expenses and financial obligations. By implementing these strategies and regularly monitoring your cash flow, you can gain a better understanding of your financial position, identify potential challenges or opportunities, and make informed decisions to optimize your cash flow management.

Consistent monitoring and proactive cash flow management will help you maintain financial stability and achieve your financial goals over time.

"it's not what you make it's what you save".

CHAPTER 2: TIPS TO SUCCEED IN BUSINESS

2.1 Define Your Unique Selling Proposition (USP):

Learn how to differentiate your business from competitors by identifying your USP and leveraging it to attract customers and drive growth. unique selling proposition revolves around providing efficient, personalized, and proactive support to customer.

The Unique Selling Proposition (USP) in a profit and loss statement refers to the specific value or benefit that sets a company's products or services apart from its competitors.

It highlights what makes the company unique and why customers should choose its offerings over others.

Incorporating the USP in a profit and loss statement can help emphasize the company's competitive advantage and showcase how it translates into financial success.

This can be achieved by showcasing how the USP contributes to revenue generation, cost savings, or overall profitability. By clearly articulating the USP in the profit and loss statement, stakeholders can better understand the impact of the company's competitive advantage on its financial results.

This alignment can also help in reinforcing the brand's positioning and differentiation in the market, ultimately driving sustainable growth and profitability.

Some Key financial metrics influenced by incorporating the Unique Selling Proposition (USP) into a profit and loss statement include:

1. Revenue Growth: The USP can drive increased sales and customer acquisition, leading to revenue growth. By highlighting how the USP attracts and retains customers, the profit and loss statement can demonstrate the impact on top-line performance.

2. Profit Margins: A strong USP can justify premium pricing, improving profit margins. By showcasing how the USP differentiates the company's products or services in the market, the profit and loss statement can illustrate the profitability impact.

3. Cost Efficiency: The USP may also lead to cost savings through operational efficiencies or reduced marketing expenses. By quantifying the cost benefits associated with the USP, the profit and loss statement can reflect improved cost efficiency.

4. Return on Investment (ROI): Incorporating the USP into financial reporting can help assess the ROI of marketing campaigns, product development, or other initiatives tied to the unique value proposition. This analysis can inform future investment decisions.

The UPS can influence customer loyalty and repeat purchases impacting the Customer Lifetime Value (CLV). by linking th UPS to customer retention and long-term value the profit and loss statement can highlight the importance on unique value proposition in driving sustainable revenue streams.

A compelling USP can help expand market share by attracting new customers and differentiating the company from competitors. By showcasing how the USP drives market penetration and customer acquisition, the profit and loss statement can reflect the company's competitive position.

The USP plays a vital role in building brand equity and consumer perception. By highlighting how the

USP resonates with target audiences and enhances brand value, the profit and loss statement can capture the intangible asset of brand equity.

A strong USP can lower customer acquisition costs (CAC) by improving conversion rates and increasing customer retention. By analyzing the impact of the USP on CAC, the profit and loss statement can demonstrate the efficiency of marketing and sales efforts.

The USP can also impact employee motivation, engagement, and productivity. By showcasing how the USP aligns with the company's values and mission, the profit and loss statement can reflect the positive influence on employee performance and organizational culture.

By integrating the USP into financial reporting, businesses can highlight their competitive advantage and differentiation strategy. The profit and loss statement can communicate how the USP positions the company uniquely in the market and contributes to sustainable growth and profitability.

With key financial metrics using the Unique Selling Proposition in the profit and loss statement, business can effectively communicate the strategic value of their competitive advantage and its impact on financial performance.

2.2 Build Strong Customer Relationships:

Understand the significance of customer satisfaction and loyalty, and discover techniques to enhance customer experience, foster long-term relationships, and generate repeat business.

Building strong customer relationships is essential for business success and can have a significant impact on financial performance. Here are some key strategies to strengthen customer relationships:

1. Personalization: Tailoring products, services, and communications to meet individual customer needs and preferences can enhance the customer experience and foster loyalty.

2. Communication: Regular and transparent communication with customers, whether through email, social media, or other channels, helps build trust and keeps customers engaged.

3. Customer Service: Providing excellent customer service, resolving issues promptly, and going the extra mile to meet customer expectations can leave a positive impression and create loyal customers.

4. Feedback and Listening: Actively seeking feedback from customers and listening to their suggestions, concerns, and preferences can help improve products, services,

and overall customer experience.

5. **Loyalty Programs:** Implementing loyalty programs, rewards, and incentives can encourage repeat purchases, increase customer retention, and strengthen relationships with existing customers.

6. **Community Engagement:** Engaging with customers through events, forums, and social media platforms can build a sense of community and connection, fostering long-term relationships.

7. **Value Addition:** Providing added value through educational content, exclusive offers, or special experiences can differentiate your brand and create a deeper connection with customers.

8. **Consistency:** Consistency in delivering high-quality products, services, and experiences reinforces trust and reliability, building long-lasting relationships with customers.

With these strategies and prioritizing customer relationship-building efforts, businesses can cultivate loyal customers, drive repeat business, and ultimately improve financial performance.

"Customer who have a good experience usually pass on that information to others, whether that's through word-of-mouth, social media or other means of communication to people they know building brand loyalty"

2.3 Embrace Innovation:

Explore the importance of staying ahead of the curve by embracing innovation, adapting to market trends, and continuously improving your products, services, and process to succeeded.

Embracing innovation is also a crucial strategy to strengthen customer relationships. By adopting new technologies, processes, and ideas, businesses can stay ahead of the curve, meet evolving customer needs, and provide unique and innovative solutions that enhance the overall customer experience.

Innovation can help businesses differentiate themselves in the market, attract new customers, and retain existing ones by offering cutting-edge products and services that add value and create memorable experiences.

Embracing innovation in profit and loss (P&L) management involves leveraging creative solutions and strategies to drive revenue growth, optimize costs, and maximize profitability. Here's how innovation can impact P&L management:

1. Revenue Growth: Innovation can help businesses identify new revenue streams, launch innovative products or services, enter new markets, and differentiate themselves from competitors. By continuously innovating and adapting to changing customer needs and market trends, businesses can drive top-line growth and increase revenue.

2. Cost Optimization: Innovation can also play a key role in optimizing costs and improving operational efficiency. By implementing innovative technologies, processes, and strategies, businesses can streamline operations, reduce waste, automate manual tasks, and lower expenses. This can have a direct impact on the bottom line and contribute to improved profitability.

3. Risk Management: Innovation in P&L management can

help businesses identify and mitigate risks that may impact financial performance. By embracing innovative risk assessment tools, predictive analytics, and scenario planning, businesses can proactively manage risks, protect profitability, and ensure financial stability.

4. Performance Monitoring: Innovations in data analytics, reporting tools, and performance metrics can provide real-time insights into the financial health of the business. By leveraging innovative dashboards and KPIs, businesses can monitor key performance indicators, track progress against targets, and make data-driven decisions to optimize P&L performance.

5. Strategic Planning: Innovation can enhance strategic planning and decision-making processes by enabling businesses to anticipate market shifts, competitive threats, and emerging opportunities. By fostering a culture of innovation and experimentation, businesses can adapt quickly to changing circumstances, stay ahead of the curve, and drive sustainable growth.

Businesses can leverage innovation to identify and target new market opportunities for revenue growth through strategic approaches and creative initiatives.

Utilize innovative market research techniques, such as big data analytics, social media listening, and predictive analytics, to gain insights into emerging trends, customer preferences, and market gaps.

By leveraging advanced analytics tools, businesses can identify new market opportunities and target segments with untapped potential.

Innovate in customer segmentation and profiling by using AI-driven customer analytics, sentiment analysis, and customer journey mapping. By understanding customer behavior, preferences, and pain points, businesses can tailor their offerings to meet specific needs and create targeted marketing campaigns to attract new customers.

Embrace innovative technologies, such as AI, machine learning, blockchain, and IoT, to enhance market targeting capabilities. By leveraging data-driven insights, automation, and personalized experiences, businesses can reach potential customers more effectively, optimize marketing strategies, and drive revenue growth in new markets.

Foster collaborations with startups, industry disruptors, or strategic partners to access new market opportunities and co-create innovative solutions. By partnering with external stakeholders, businesses can leverage complementary strengths, share resources, and enter new markets through innovative joint ventures or alliances.

Adopt agile market entry strategies that allow for quick experimentation, validation, and adaptation in new markets. By testing minimum viable products, conducting pilot projects, and iterating based on feedback, businesses can reduce risks, accelerate market entry, and capitalize on emerging opportunities with innovative approaches.

Innovate in marketing strategies, branding initiatives, and customer engagement tactics to stand out in new markets and attract target audiences. By creating compelling storytelling, experiential marketing campaigns, and interactive content, businesses can build brand awareness, foster customer loyalty, and drive revenue growth in untapped markets.

By incorporating innovation into market identification and targeting strategies, businesses can uncover new revenue opportunities, expand their market reach, and drive sustainable growth in today's competitive business landscape.

CHAPTER 3: TIPS TO WIN IN THE FINANCIAL INDUSTRY

3.1 Stay Informed:

Keep up with the latest industry trends, regulations, and market developments to make informed decisions and seize opportunities.

Staying informed about profit and loss is essential for businesses to track financial performance, make informed decisions, and drive profitability. Here are some tips on how businesses can stay informed about profit and loss:

Financial Reporting: Regularly review and analyse financial statements, such as income statements, balance sheets, and cash flow statements, to track revenue, expenses, and profitability. Use accounting software or financial management tools to generate accurate financial reports and monitor key performance indicators (KPIs) related to profit and loss.

Budgeting and Forecasting: Develop detailed budgets and financial forecasts to plan for revenue targets, cost projections, and profit margins. Compare actual financial results against budgeted figures to identify variances, analyse trends, and make adjustments to improve profitability.

Cost Management Monitor and control costs across all aspects of the business, including production, operations, marketing, and overhead expenses. Conduct cost-benefit analyses, identify cost-saving opportunities, negotiate supplier contracts, and optimize resource allocation to maximize profitability and minimize expenses.

Evaluate pricing strategies, product margins, and pricing models to ensure optimal pricing that aligns with market demand, competitive landscape, and profit objectives. Conduct pricing analyses, assess pricing elasticity, and adjust pricing strategies based on customer feedback and market dynamics to drive profitability.

Analyze revenue streams, sales performance, customer segments, and product lines to identify revenue drivers, growth opportunities, and areas for revenue optimization. Implement sales tracking systems, customer relationship management (CRM) tools, and revenue analytics to gain insights into revenue trends and maximize revenue potential.

Calculate and monitor key profitability ratios, such as gross profit margin, net profit margin, return on investment (ROI), and return on assets (ROA), to assess financial performance and profitability. Use financial ratios to benchmark performance, compare against industry peers, and identify areas for improvement in profit and loss management.

Conduct regular financial performance reviews, financial audits, and management meetings to discuss profit and loss trends, financial challenges, and strategic initiatives to enhance profitability. Engage with financial advisors, accountants, and business consultants to gain expert insights and recommendations for optimizing profit and loss management.

Profit and Loss through financial reporting, budgeting, cost management, pricing strategies, revenue analysis, profitability ratios, and financial performance reviews, businesses can track financial health, make informed decisions, and drive sustainable profitability in today's competitive business landscape.

3.2 Develop a Strong Professional Network:

Learn how to build and nurture relationships with industry professionals, and potential clients to expand your reach and gain valuable insights.

Building a strong professional network in profit and loss management is crucial for professionals looking to enhance their financial expertise, explore opportunities in finance, and stay updated on industry trends.

Participate in industry-specific events, such as financial conferences, seminars, and workshops focused on profit and loss management. These gatherings provide opportunities to connect with finance professionals, experts in financial analysis, and leaders in profit optimization.

Become a member of financial associations or organizations that focus on profit and loss management, such as the Financial Planning Association, Association for Financial Professionals, or Chartered Institute of Management Accountants, Actively engaging with professionals in profit and loss management, you can build a strong network of contacts, gain valuable insights, and advance your finance for business success.

3.3 Continuously Enhance Your Skills:

Invest in your professional development by acquiring new skills, pursuing certifications, and staying updated with industry best practices.

Continuously enhancing your skills in profit and loss management is crucial for finance professionals seeking to excel in analyzing financial performance, optimizing profitability, and making strategic business decisions. Here are tailored strategies to help you continually improve your skills in profit and loss management:

1. Advanced Financial Analysis Courses: Enroll in advanced financial analysis courses that focus on profit and loss statements, financial ratios, cost analysis, and revenue forecasting. These courses provide in-depth knowledge and practical skills to analyze financial data, identify trends, and make informed decisions to enhance profitability.

2. Specialized Certifications: Pursue specialized certifications in financial management, such as Certified Management Accountant (CMA) or Chartered Financial Analyst (CFA), with a focus on profit and loss analysis. These certifications validate your expertise in financial analysis, budgeting, and performance evaluation, enhancing your credibility in profit and loss management.

3. Data Analytics Training: Enhance your data analytics skills by taking courses in data visualization, statistical analysis, and predictive modeling. Proficiency in data analytics enables you to extract valuable insights from financial data, identify cost-saving opportunities, and optimize profit margins through data-driven decision-making.

4. Cost Management Workshops: Attend workshops or seminars on cost management strategies, variance analysis, and budget control to strengthen your skills in cost optimization and expense management. Understanding cost structures, cost drivers, and budgeting techniques is essential for effective profit and loss management.

5. **Continuous Industry Research:** Stay updated on industry trends, regulatory changes, and market dynamics impacting profit and loss management in your sector. Regularly read industry reports, financial publications, and market analyses to deepen your understanding of key factors influencing profitability and financial performance.

6. **Mentorship from Finance Experts:** Seek mentorship from experienced finance professionals specializing in profit and loss management to gain valuable insights, guidance, and best practices. Mentors can provide feedback on your analysis techniques, recommend strategies for improving profitability, and share real-world experiences to enhance your skills.

7. **Participate in Case Studies and Simulations:** Engage in case studies, simulations, or business games focused on profit and loss scenarios to practice applying financial analysis concepts in a simulated environment. Hands-on experience in analyzing financial data, making strategic decisions, and measuring performance outcomes can sharpen your skills in profit and loss management.

By leveraging these tailored strategies and actively investing in profit and loss management, you can enhance your analytical capabilities, decision-making skills, and strategic acumen in driving financial success for your business.

The key to making money is to ensure your revenue exceeds your expenses. It's like a game of balancing your check book, but with a twist. So, instead of being a "loss"er, channel your inner "profit"eer and make those numbers work in your favour!

Summary:

Congratulations! You have now gained valuable insights into mastering profit and loss, succeeding in business, and excelling in the financial industry. By implementing these top tips, you will be well-equipped to balance the books, drive profitability, and achieve long-term financial success. Remember, success requires dedication, continuous learning, and adaptability. So, go out there, apply these strategies, and make your mark in the world of finance!

ABOUT THE AUTHOR

Cora Ferguson

Thank you for supporting my vision that i had for a while which has finally taken shape.

I am a mother of two wonderful boys who motivate me every day to always aim for the stars.

I have worked within the Retail Sector for over 15 years managing different Luxury Department Store, this has allowed me to gain valuable experience in different areas of Business and therefore I hope with the Top Tips within this book you will be able to balance your Profit and Loss books to acquire financial success within your Business.

Thanks and God Bless.

www.ingramcontent.com/pod-product-compliance
Lightning Source LLC
Chambersburg PA
CBHW071001220526
45471CB00007B/3127